Astronomy Now!™

A Look at
NEPTUNE

Suzanne Slade

PowerKiDS press.
New York

With love to Al and Lois Snipes

Published in 2008 by The Rosen Publishing Group, Inc.
29 East 21st Street, New York, NY 10010

First Edition

Editor: Amelie von Zumbusch
Book Design: Greg Tucker
Photo Researcher: Nicole Pristash

Photo Credits: Cover, p. 13 (main) © Photodisc; p. 5 (main) © NASA; pp. 5 (inset), 11, 15 (main), 15 (top) © Getty Images; p. 7 (main) © Shutterstock.com; p. 7 (inset) © Digital Vision; p. 9 © Lunar and Planetary Institute; p. 13 (inset) © NASA Kennedy Space Center (NASA-KSC); pp. 17 (main), 19 Courtesy NASA/JPL-Caltech; p. 21 © NASA/Roger Ressmeyer/CORBIS.

Library of Congress Cataloging-in-Publication Data

Slade, Suzanne.
  A look at Neptune / Suzanne Slade. — 1st ed.
     p. cm. — (Astronomy now!)
  Includes index.
  ISBN-13: 978-1-4042-3832-9 (library binding)
  ISBN-10: 1-4042-3832-8 (library binding)
  1. Neptune (Planet)—Juvenile literature. I. Title.
  QB691.S63 2008
  523.48'1—dc22
                                    2007011804

Manufactured in the United States of America

Contents

Naming Neptune

Astronomers found nearly all the planets in our solar system by chance. The one exception to this is the planet Neptune. Astronomers used math to guess where Neptune could be found. In 1846, astronomer Johann Gottfried Galle became the first person to see Neptune. Through his telescope, Neptune looked like a dim spot of light about the size of a piece of sugar.

The astronomer Urbain Le Verrier suggested naming this newest planet Neptune, after the Roman god of the sea. Le Verrier followed the common practice of naming planets after Roman or Greek gods.

The planet Neptune is known for its deep blue color. *Inset:* Astronomers came up with several other names before deciding to name Neptune after the Roman god of the sea, seen here.

5

A Far-Out Planet

Neptune is our solar system's eighth planet from the Sun. About 2.8 **billion** miles (4.5 billion km) lie between Neptune and the Sun. Neptune travels around the Sun in an oval path. This path is called its orbit. It takes Neptune about 165 years to make one full orbit around the Sun.

Neptune also spins much like a top. The amount of time it takes a planet to spin once is the length of its day. Neptune spins around once every 16 hours and 7 minutes, so its day is a little over 16 hours long.

Neptune is farther from the Sun than any other planet in our solar system.
Inset: Neptune takes longer to orbit the Sun than any other planet. This is because it is the farthest planet from the Sun.

Big and Blue

Neptune is so large that about 60 Earths could fit inside it. This huge planet is mostly made of different gases. However, it has a hard core, or center, of melted rock that is about the size of Earth. This core makes heat. Unlike Earth, Neptune makes more heat than it gets from the Sun.

A blanket of gases, called an **atmosphere**, covers Neptune. Although no one has visited Neptune, its atmosphere is believed to be more than three-quarters **hydrogen** gas. This atmosphere also has small amounts of **helium** and **methane** gas. The methane helps give Neptune its bright blue color.

Atmosphere

Mantle

Core

Scientists think that a layer, or level, of liquid hydrogen, called the mantle, lies between Neptune's core and its atmosphere. You can see Neptune's core, mantle, and atmosphere in this drawing.

A Stormy Planet

Scientists have discovered many storms in Neptune's atmosphere. The spacecraft *Voyager 2*'s visit to Neptune in 1989 let scientists study these storms. They named one small, fast storm the Scooter. The Scooter traveled all the way around Neptune in just 16 hours!

Scientists also discovered a storm on the southern half of Neptune. The storm was about the size of Earth. Scientists named it the Great Dark Spot. The storm moved at about 700 miles per hour (1,127 km/h)! When scientists looked for the storm again in 1994, it had disappeared. However, they found another big storm in the planet's northern half.

You can see the Great Dark Spot and the Scooter in this picture of Neptune, taken by *Voyager 2*. You can also see another big storm, called Dark Spot 2.

The Great Dark Spot

The Scooter

Dark Spot 2

Cool Facts

Neptune is the fourth-largest planet in our solar system.

If you were to visit Neptune, you would not be able to stand on this planet since it is made of flowing gases.

The winds in Neptune's atmosphere travel more than 1,200 miles per hour (2,000 km/h).

As Neptune orbits the Sun, the closest it ever comes to Earth is 2.7 billion miles (4.3 billion km) away.

A year on Neptune lasts as long as 165 years on Earth.

A Neptune Timeline

1989 – The spacecraft *Voyager 2* flies by Neptune and studies the planet.

1949 – Astronomer Gerard Kuiper finds Nereid, Neptune's third-biggest moon.

1846 – William Lassell spots Neptune's biggest moon, Triton, on October 10.

1846 – Johann Gottfried Galle uses Urbain Le Verrier's math to find Neptune with a telescope, on September 23.

Neptune's Moons

Neptune's biggest moon, Triton, is round. However, many of the planet's smaller moons, such as Proteus, Thalassa, and Despina, have irregular, or uneven, shapes.

Neptune's closest moon is named Naiad. It takes Naiad about 7 hours to orbit Neptune.

Neptune's moon Nereid has the most uneven orbit of any moon in our solar system. Nereid can be as close as 841,100 miles (1.35 million km) or as far as 6 million miles (9.6 million km) from Neptune.

Finding Neptune

In the 1800s, astronomers noticed that the planet Uranus did not orbit the Sun in the path they expected. Some astronomers, such as John Couch Adams, in England, and Urbain Le Verrier, in France, thought that another planet past Uranus was causing this strange orbit.

Le Verrier and Adams used math to guess where this planet would be. Le Verrier passed his math along to a German astronomer named Johann Gottfried Galle. In 1846, Galle searched the sky with his telescope and found this new planet. It was exactly where Le Verrier said it would be!

John Couch Adams

Johann Gottfried Galle

Urbain Le Verrier

Scientists work together to make discoveries about our solar system. Adams, Le Verrier, Galle, and other scientists who worked with them all played a part in the discovery of Neptune.

Neptune's Moons

Neptune's **gravity** holds many moons in orbit around it. So far, scientists have found 13 moons orbiting Neptune. Six of these were discovered in 1989, when the spacecraft *Voyager 2* flew past Neptune.

Neptune's largest moon is called Triton. This moon was first spotted in 1846, by the British astronomer William Lassell. He found Triton just 17 days after Neptune was discovered. Neptune's third-largest moon, Nereid, was found next, in 1949. Proteus, the planet's second-largest moon, was not discovered until later because it was too dark to be seen through the telescopes of that time.

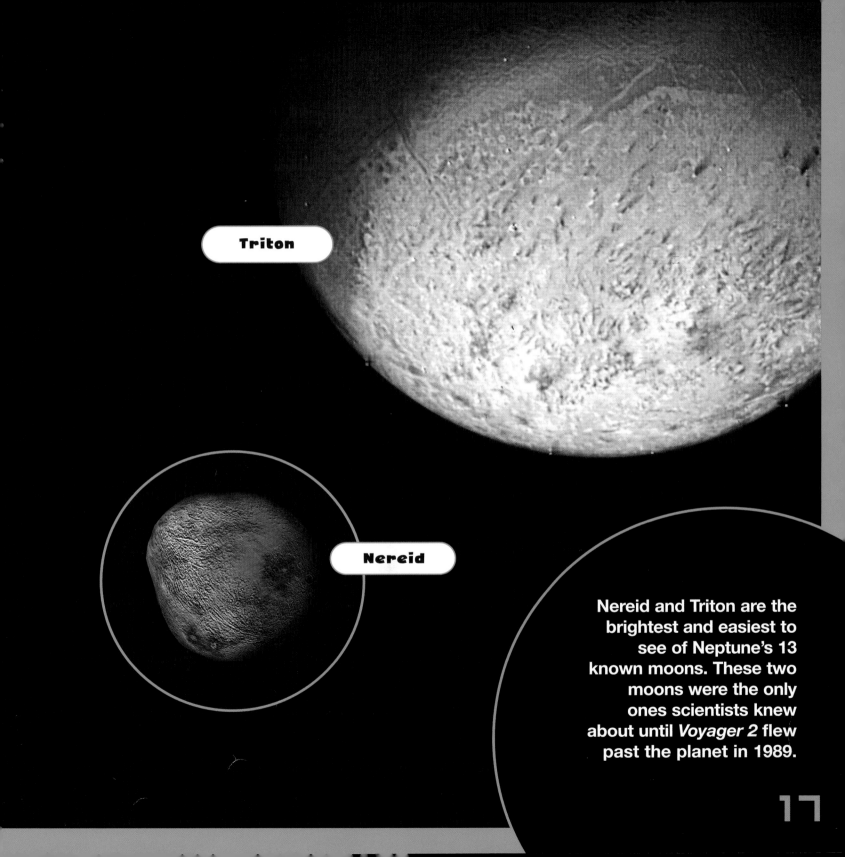

Triton

Nereid

Nereid and Triton are the brightest and easiest to see of Neptune's 13 known moons. These two moons were the only ones scientists knew about until *Voyager 2* flew past the planet in 1989.

17

Mighty Triton

Measuring 1,680 miles (2,704 km) across, Triton is half the width of the planet Mercury. Triton is the only big moon in the solar system that orbits backward. This means Triton orbits Neptune in the **opposite** direction that Neptune orbits the Sun.

This mighty moon is the coldest place in the solar system. Triton can be as cold as -391° F (-235° C). It is mostly covered with ice. Triton's outside has both smooth places and places broken by long, deep lines. *Voyager 2* took pictures that show **nitrogen** gas and dust shooting out from Triton into the moon's very thin atmosphere.

Triton's thin atmosphere is made mostly of nitrogen. Triton is one of just three known solar system objects with a nitrogen atmosphere. The other two are Saturn's moon Titan and our own planet Earth.

Mystery Rings

Neptune is also circled by rings. These rings have raised many questions. They were a mystery to astronomers for many years because no one could see if the rings went all the way around Neptune. *Voyager 2* answered this question when it took pictures showing that Neptune had several rings. The brightest of these rings were named Galle, Le Verrier, Lassell, Arago, and Adams, after important scientists.

Voyager 2 found that parts of the Adams ring were brighter than the rest of the ring. These parts are called ring arcs. Like the rest of Neptune's rings, the ring arcs are made of dust and rocks.

Voyager 2 took this picture of Neptune's rings. The Le Verrier ring is on the inside, and the Adams ring is on the outside. The thick, bright parts of the Adams ring are the ring arcs.

What's Next on Neptune?

Much of what we know about Neptune and its rings and moons comes from *Voyager 2*'s 1989 visit there. Scientists use a powerful telescope called the Hubble Space Telescope to study Neptune, too. In the years ahead, scientists hope to discover more about Neptune's powerful storms and strange weather. They want to find out why certain bands of weather form around the planet's middle, just as they do in Earth's atmosphere.

Plans have been made for another spacecraft to blast off for Neptune in 2035. Until then, scientists will keep using telescopes to learn more about this interesting blue planet.

Glossary

astronomers (uh-STRAH-nuh-merz) People who study the Sun, the Moon, the planets, and the stars.

atmosphere (AT-muh-sfeer) The gases around an object in space.

billion (BIL-yun) A thousand millions.

gravity (GRA-vih-tee) The force that causes objects to move toward each other. The bigger an object is, the more gravity it has.

helium (HEE-lee-um) A light, colorless gas.

hydrogen (HY-dreh-jen) A colorless gas that burns easily and weighs less than any other known kind of matter.

methane (MEH-thayn) A gas that burns easily.

nitrogen (NY-truh-jen) A gas without taste or color that can be found in the air.

opposite (O-puh-zet) Totally and exactly different.

scientists (SY-un-tists) People who study the world.

solar system (SOH-ler SIS-tem) A group of planets that circles a star.

telescope (TEH-leh-skohp) A tool used to make faraway objects appear closer and larger.

Index

Web Sites

Due to the changing nature of Internet links, PowerKids Press has developed an online list of Web sites related to the subject of this book. This site is updated regularly. Please use this link to access the list: www.powerkidslinks.com/astro/neptune/